JUNIOR BIOGRAPHIES

Kristen Rajczak Nelson

JEFFERSON DAVIS

LEADER OF THE CONFEDERACY

Enslow Publishing
101 W. 23rd Street
Suite 240
New York, NY 10011
USA
enslow.com

Words to Know

citizen A person who lives in a country and has all the rights of that country.

Confederacy The Southern states during the Civil War.

elect To choose someone for a government position.

plantation A large farm.

publish To print and sell a book or other written work.

represent To stand for a group of people.

resign To leave a job or office.

secede To leave an organization or country.

senator A person in the government who represents a certain area, like a state.

surrender To give up fighting.

troop A group of soldiers.

Union The Northern states during the Civil War.

Contents

Jefferson Davis

CHAPTER 1
EARLY LIFE

Jefferson Davis was born on June 3 in 1807 or 1808. His family lived in Kentucky when he was born. A few years later they moved to Mississippi. Jefferson was the youngest of ten children. His parents were Samuel and Jane Davis. Samuel had served in the American Revolution. Jefferson's family were farmers. They had a **plantation**. Still, they didn't have a lot of money.

SCHOOL DAYS

Jefferson's brother, Joseph, was much older than he was. Joseph helped his young brother. He paid for him to go to school. Jefferson went to Transylvania University in Kentucky.

Jefferson Davis Says:

"Truthfulness is a cornerstone in character, and if it be not firmly laid in youth, there will ever after be a weak spot in the foundation."

A view of West Point, the school that Jefferson attended for four years

In 1824, he started attending the US Military Academy at West Point. Jefferson was not a great student there. He finished in 1828. He then became an officer in the US Army.

Davis went to Illinois and Wisconsin with the army. Zachary Taylor was in charge of his group. Taylor later

became president of the United States. In 1833, Davis met Taylor's daughter, Sarah. The two fell in love. Sarah's father was not happy. Davis left the army in 1835 to marry Sarah. But both Davis and his wife got ill. Sarah died about three months after their wedding.

As a young man, Jefferson Davis was a soldier in the army. He followed in the footsteps of his father and uncles, who were soldiers in the Revolutionary War.

A SECOND CHANCE

Davis started a plantation in Mississippi. It was called Brierfield. It was

Jefferson Davis with his second wife, Varina. She came from a wealthy Mississippi family.

Davis and Varina had six children, two girls and four boys.

a cotton plantation. Davis used slaves to work in his fields. He thought slavery was important. It was a big part of life in the South.

Davis decided to run for a job in the government. In 1845, he was **elected** to the US House of Representatives. He **represented** Mississippi. That same year, Davis married Varina Howell.

Chapter 2
Davis in Politics

Davis was in the House of Representatives for less than a year. In 1846, the Mexican-American War began. Davis **resigned** from his job. He became a colonel. He led soldiers in the war. Again, Davis served under Zachary Taylor. Davis led **troops** from Mississippi. They won the Battle of Monterrey. He also helped the troops win at the Battle of Buena Vista. Davis was hurt during the battle.

Becoming a Leader

In 1847, Davis returned to the government. This time he was a **senator** for Mississippi. He ran for governor of Mississippi in 1851. He did not win. In 1853, President Franklin Pierce made Davis secretary of war. He did well at his job. President Pierce left office in 1857. Davis became a senator again.

Jefferson Davis Says:

"I love the Union and the Constitution, but I would rather leave the Union with the Constitution than remain in the Union without it."

A battle in the Mexican-American War. The United States wanted to expand the country. It fought Mexico to get more land.

Franklin Pierce was the fourteenth president of the United States. He made Davis secretary of war in 1853.

NORTH VERSUS SOUTH

At this time, the Northern and Southern states were divided. They disagreed about many things. One of these was slavery. Davis and the Southern states supported slavery. The Northern states believed slavery was wrong. Abraham Lincoln was elected president in 1861. He told people he would end slavery. Southern states wanted to **secede**. They did not want to be part of the **Union**. Davis wanted to keep the Union together. Still, he believed the states had the right to secede.

Many people believe that Davis did not want the job of president of the Confederacy.

In January 1861, Mississippi seceded from the Union. Davis resigned from the Senate. He was made commander of the army in Mississippi. Then, on February 18, 1861, he was made president of the new Confederate States of America.

A crowd gathers to watch Davis's inauguration in 1861. The inauguration took place in Montgomery, Alabama, the first capital of the Confederacy.

Chapter 3
Civil War Failure

At first, the people of the South were in favor of President Davis. He was a strong army leader. He had been a member of Congress. And he believed in Southern values. But Davis didn't stay popular for long. The people in his government fought with each other. Davis didn't like when people disagreed with him. And he put leaders in place who didn't do well at their jobs. What's more, the Confederate army was failing. It had too few soldiers, and too little food, clothing, and guns. During this time, Davis was often ill.

End of the War

By April 1865, Davis knew that the war was almost over. Union troops were getting ready to capture Richmond, Virginia. Richmond was the capital of the **Confederacy**.

Jefferson Davis Says:

"We are not fighting for slavery. We are fighting for Independence."

President Davis sits with the members of his cabinet.

It was also the Davis family's home. Davis gave his wife some gold. He told her to use it to keep herself and their children safe.

The first Confederate flag with thirteen stars. They stand for the eleven states that left the Union, plus Kentucky and Missouri.

Davis and others in his government left Richmond. Hours later, the Union Army arrived and took the city. Davis was able to keep away from the Union troops for a little more than a month. But by May, Union soldiers caught up with Davis. He was captured in Georgia.

CHARGED AND JAILED

Davis was taken to Fort Monroe in Virginia.

This photo shows Union soldiers around an ambulance carrying Davis after his capture.

He was charged with the crime of treason. This means a **citizen** has tried to overthrow the government of his own country. Davis was in prison for two years. He was released in 1867.

General Robert E. Lee surrendered to Union troops at the Battle of Appomattox Court House. But President Davis hadn't approved it!

Chapter 4
After the War

After jail, Davis returned to his wife and children. They traveled to Canada and parts of the United States. They visited with people like Robert E. Lee. Davis never stood trial for treason. The charges against him were dropped after a time.

A New Life

In 1868, the Davis family set out for Europe. They hoped that the change would improve his health. They returned in October 1869. Davis began looking for a job. He took a job with an insurance company for a few years. He even became its president. During this time, the Davis family lived a few places in the South. The company did not do well. Davis resigned in 1873.

Davis lost his US citizenship at the end of the war. He got it back in 1978.

Davis around 1865. He spent two years in prison without ever having a trial.

Davis sits with his wife, daughter, and grandchildren at their home in Mississippi around 1885.

FINAL YEARS

Jefferson Davis moved back to Mississippi. Some people wanted him to run for Congress again. But Davis had been charged with treason. So he was not allowed to run for office. Instead, he worked to move Confederate soldiers from wartime graves to proper cemeteries. He also worked on a book about his time as head

A statue of Davis stands at his grave in Richmond, Virginia.

of the Confederacy. *The Rise and Fall of the Confederate Government* was **published** as two books in 1881.

On December 6, 1889, Jefferson Davis died in New Orleans, Louisiana. More than 200,000 people came to his burial in New Orleans. In 1893, he was reburied in Richmond, Virginia.

Jefferson Davis Says:

"You will see many errors to forgive, many deficiencies to tolerate...but you shall not find in me either a want of zeal or fidelity to the cause."

Timeline

1807 or 1808 Jefferson Davis is born on June 3.

1828 Finishes school at West Point.

1845 Marries Varina Banks Howell.

Is elected to the House of Representatives.

1846 Resigns from the House to serve in the Mexican-American War.

1853–1857 Serves as secretary of war under President Franklin Pierce.

1861 Becomes the president of the Confederate States of America.

1865 Is captured by Union troops and taken to Fort Monroe.

1867 Released from Fort Monroe.

1881 *The Rise and Fall of the Confederate Government* is published.

1889 Jefferson Davis dies on December 6.

1978 Davis's citizenship is restored.

1998 The Jefferson Davis Presidential Library opens in Biloxi, Mississippi.

2012 Most recent volume of *The Papers of Jefferson Davis* is published.

Learn More

Books

Doeden, Matt. *The Civil War: An Interactive History Adventure.* Mankato, MN: Capstone Press, 2016.

Mara, Will, and Roger Zanni. *If You Were a Kid During the Civil War.* New York, NY: Children's Press, 2016.

Roxburgh, Ellis. *Abraham Lincoln vs. Jefferson Davis: Presidents of a Divided Nation.* New York, NY: Gareth Stevens Publishing, 2016.

Websites

America's Story: Civil War

www.americaslibrary.gov/jb/civil/jb_civil_davis_1.html

Check out a timeline of the Civil War, including when Jefferson Davis was elected president of the Confederacy.

What Everyone Should Know About the Civil War

www.civilwar.org/learn/articles/10-facts-what-everyone-should-know-about-civil-war

Review ten of the most important facts about the Civil War on this website.

Index

Published in 2019 by Enslow Publishing, LLC.
101 W. 23rd Street, Suite 240, New York, NY 10011

Library of Congress Cataloging-in-Publication Data

Names: Rajczak Nelson, Kristen, author.
Title: Jefferson Davis : Leader of the Confederacy / Kristen Rajczak Nelson.
Description: New York : Enslow Publishing, 2019. | Series: Junior biographies
Audience: Grades 3-5. | Includes bibliographical references and index.
Identifiers: LCCN 2018004956| ISBN 9781978502031 (library bound) | ISBN 9781978502949 (pbk.) | ISBN 9781978502956 (6 pack)
Subjects: LCSH: Davis, Jefferson, 1808-1889—Juvenile literature. | Presidents—Confederate States of America—Biography—Juvenile literature.
Classification: LCC E467.1.D26 R34 2019 | DDC 973.7/13092 [B] —dc23
LC record available at https://lccn.loc.gov/2018004956

Printed in the United States of America

To Our Readers: We have done our best to make sure all website addresses in this book were active and appropriate when we went to press. However, the author and the publisher have no control over and assume no liability for the material available on those websites or on any websites they may link to. Any comments or suggestions can be sent by e-mail to customerservice@enslow.com.

Photos Credits: Cover, p. 1 Stock Montage/Archive Photos/Getty Images; pp. 2, 3, 22, 23, 24, back cover (curves graphic) Alena Kazlouskaya/Shutterstock.com; pp. 4, 15, 20 Library of Congress Prints and Photographs Division Washington, DC; p. 6 Shelburne Museum, Vermont, USA/Museum purchase, acquired from Maxim Karolik/Bridgeman Images; p. 7 Buyenlarge/Archive Photos/Getty Images; p. 8 Science History Images/Alamy Stock Photo; p. 11 Universal Images Group/Getty Images; pp. 12, 19 Hulton Archive/Getty Images; p. 13 © AP Images; p. 16 Sheridan Libraries/Levy/Gado/Archive Photos/Getty Images; p. 17 Corbis Historical/Getty Images; p. 21 Andrew Lichtenstein/Corbis News/Getty Images; interior page bottoms (Civil War scene) kstudija/Shutterstock.com.